DRINKING THE RIVER

Drinking the River

POEMS

David Polk

FOMITE

Copyright © 2021 David Polk

All rights reserved.
No part of this book may be reproduced in any form or by any means without the prior written consent of the publisher, except in the case of brief quotations used in reviews and certain other noncommercial uses permitted by copyright law.

ISBN-13-978-1-947917 64 4
Library of Congress Number: 2020947109

The author wishes to thank the Kentucky Arts Council for a grant in support of his work.

Fomite
58 Peru Street
Burlington, VT 05401
www.fomitepress.com

TO MY SON

The River

"It is serenely and silently not subject—to us or to anything else except the other natural forces that are also beyond our control."

—Wendell Berry

The Animals

"What were the secrets of the animal's likeness with, and unlikeness from, man? The secrets whose existence man recognized as soon as he intercepted an animal's look. All the secrets were about animals as an *intercession* between man and his origin."

—John Berger

Contents

At the Edge 1

Canoe on the Ohio 3

First Ride Mowing in Spring 4

Cloudless Spring Sky 6

Water Moccasin 7

Coyote at Dusk 8

Tale of a Frog 9

No-Man's-Land, Mid-Summer 10

Owl 12

Underneath 14

At the Window 15

In the Orchard 16

The Blue-Tailed Skink 17

Winter on the Cumberland 18

Gulls in Winter Light 19

The Backyard, Late Winter 21

Raking in Late March 22

At Home, Sick, But Feeling Better 24

At Lusk Creek Canyon 25

Open Secret 27

The Ohio at Smithland 29

A World 31

Flood　33

June Rain　35

Summer Midnight　37

Meeting after Weeks of Separation　39

Trail　41

The Wife　43

Turkey Vultures　45

Watery Days　46

A Meaningless Creek Pebble　48

The Roof　49

Burred, Mute Stray Dog　50

Mandala　52

Quick Red Squirrel Cartoon　53

Out of the Half World　55

On a Walk to the Supermarket　59

No Help　60

The Deer of Seven Mile Creek　61

Death of a Mouse　62

Crows　64

February Cold Front　66

A Vole in March Snow　67

In the Rockies　68

Jonquils　69

The Beast　70

After a Near Fatal Illness　71

The Old Mayfield Road　72

Trumpet Vines of Shawnee Island   75
Thunderstorm   76
Mourning Doves   80
Here and There   84
North Atlantic Herring   85
Figs   86
Watching TV with Mother…   88
The Seeping Dream   89
Blue Wasps in November   91
What the River Contains   93

At the Edge

1. At Six Years Old

In April, the rain-swollen creek
surged with muddy milk. Left behind,
its warm summer pools were still.
On my knees, I studied a quiet shallow.
What lived in the green water hid,
what swam in it like shadows.
An egg-round stone, half-buried claw:
what one found there was in place
loosely, briefly, yet fit absolutely.
A slender minnow materialized
near the surface: a translucent wisp.
It fled, returned, halted before me,
levitated in the pool and in my mind.

Fall rains filled it, brimmed, over-ran.
Sworn to keep a distance, I crawled
closer, magnetized, inched my way
within reach of its frothy plunging,
its furious, limb-dragging speed.
I was spray-soaked, no matter, riveted—
thrilled to feel the pure negation.
The November high eddied away
toward what? I didn't know to ask.

II. *At Seven*

Where the creeks slowed and emptied,
forfeited their shape and simple light,
the river — the Ohio — is a mile wide.
We stopped on an after-church drive
where the tilt down to it began — the tug
into it the car brakes groaned against.
Twiglike trees stood along the far shore.

I stood among driftwood at the brink.
I breathed in its cool air, rich with decay.
It moved all over. Was it slow or fast?
A water so wide sheds quick takes.
Its odor, like my own repelled, attracted.
The Major — father's friend — had swum
across and must be, I thought, unsinkable.
Mother said we drink it every day.
It was more though than only water.
I dipped it with a paper cup: what held
still there one knew was not river.
It was all forward: ahead and behind itself.
It lapped ashore on the boat-ramp stone,
small waves lapped. I crouched there
in the monotony of the timeless
where a child is keenly at home.

Canoe on the Ohio

May rains: both rivers are filled and rising.
The muddy water churns, alive under me.
I'm in retreat, unnerved, then it happens:
a strand of the Ohio, higher, stronger, flows
into the Cumberland's mouth. It sweeps me
with it suddenly: counter current yards wide
it runs swiftly along the bank and takes me
upstream, incredulous, as in the luft dream
where I glide on arm-wings if I do not ask
how or for how long the burden of earth law
can be suspended. It loses force, plays out
near the bridge. The boat slows, confronted,
and turns again downstream. But I've taken
a full erotic jolt — giddy as I paddle home.

First Ride Mowing in Spring

The motor refuses, stutters, does catch,
and I sweep down shaggy meadow now.
The gold of dandelions is cheap.
I'm chopping wild onion, releasing scent.
A soft limb gets axed; up jumps a rabbit.
A patch of henbit — little pagodas levelled.
Deep grass along the fence row
chokes the mower, and I climb down —
clear the moist gobbets underneath.
Two wary crows browse in my wake.
The air gusts cold, yet the sun
asserts itself — its superior claim.

The backyard is crowded with grass,
the black earth feeds its green appetite.
Chilly rain soaked it yesterday,
now each slender leaf angles
for its full measure of light.
New peony stalks are knee-high
in their ill-defined bed.
White flowers flushed-pink
will in May swell themselves open
and yield to my lustful eye.

I swing around again. Peony stalks
look feathery, a brownish red.
They thrash about in the whirlwind
of blade and exhaust. Then —
skirting a stone — I cut too close.

Cloudless Spring Sky

The pair of swallows pasted their mud nest
under the porch eave — I allowed them.
They dive on me now bald babies crowd it.
Even this pleases as I hurry for the door.
With the barn cousins, they hunt the air
over the lush creek bottom: rise and sail
through the empty space that is time.
I spy on the five infants, weak chirpers —
the legacy, alive one hour to the next.
One thrusts its maw higher and stares
into the air, closes, opens. They wait
beneath the day's blue, cloudless sky.
A swallow can spot a raindrop — catch
it in its open mouth. It packs its throat
with flies, bees and moths for the young.
They didn't return, the eave parents.
Nothing could stop them if they lived.
And I was of no use, no one could be.

Water Moccasin

The canoe coasts up the creek mouth
into a green light of leafy trees.
An essence left by receding river
coats the trunks and lower branches.
A silence pervades, and yet withholds.
I scrape below in shallow water and
a long-fallen sycamore, a tangle of
bony limbs and roots blocks passage.
The reek is of algae and fertile dregs.
In this uninhibited, bottomland pocket
if no snake had ever been, the place itself
would clot — would congeal into one,
and it is there on the bank beside me
where I saw nothing before: the thick S
of water moccasin, its cryptic dun-drab,
its spear-head face, the innocent eyes.
When it strikes only a blur is seen in
recall: white vise of the open mouth.

I back paddle. Quietly remove myself
to the river: its wide sweep, airy breath.
The water's flooded with light. Current
takes the canoe again. I need only ride,
relieved by the blue of late morning,
the uncreated clarity of summer sky.

Coyote at Dusk

He's quick-eyed in the dim maze of thicket and cane.
Emerging now, he dips his nose in damp grass
glazed with essence of man-child where I passed.
Is one the odd soup of scents: urine salts and soap
blown across a field, a riddle and menace of air?
'An upright one,' he concludes, 'one who learned
to walk on flowers and leaves of Persian carpet.'
He crosses the bean field with purpose, his neck
loose between the lean shoulders, his brisk motion
an elegant integration of stride and awareness.
He glances to the far ridge: yellow light opens
a window in the dusk. From head to tail, he listens:
the radiant piano of a Mozart sonata reaches him
and my rapt hum-along. He savors; he considers.
'Overly consonant, yet danceable,' he decides
and accelerating, trots on into the hungry night.

Tale of a Frog

In a fury of self, I think to destroy the frog
whose fault I say it is I cannot sleep.
He's on the porch. I spot him in flashlight:
a legged, small lump — shadowy tan,
the color exactly of the worst clay soil.
I clap a plastic sandwich bag over him.
The pale throat sac with which he sounded
five times larger hangs loose, thumping fast.
The star-shaped feet suction to the bag's side,
splayed, hand-like feet. Even the bulging eyes'
color is camouflage, part of his earth mask.
Here before the ur-people, he has no idea.

I free him among the shadowy bean plants.
Switch off my light in the moonless dark.
He's motionless. He risks no comment.
Night in the creek-bottom field is warm,
its odor of germination, moist foliage.
I am a menacing giant, or is it merciful?
In a fairy tale, two frogs might debate it,
but no one rules here at this hour. And I go.
He will find his midnight voice again.

No-Man's Land, Mid-Summer

The Ohio at mid-morning: the great clearing it makes.
Walking down to it, breaking stride, one can feel how
small rivers are for miles pulled to its enormous bed.
Its water is opaque, unreadable, a palest tan tinged
with algae green and slathered with the blue of day.
I push off in the canoe: out onto the glittering flats —
the live, supple, far-spreading sameness of it all.
Quickly then the bank recedes: thrilling, sobering.
Wind, boat-wake can swamp you. Turbulence rises
from the depths, roils and plays out and subsides.
A blue heron rides a flotsam raft downstream.
Above me swallows fling themselves awry, glide
at ease with the shifting surface beneath them.
I'm overtaking long and lopsided Shawnee Island.
Unearthed trees lie beached on its sandy point,
roots tangled in bare branches. The swallows nest
high in the cliff face. The river works away at it
below and will in time bring it down into itself.
Some big bright thing suddenly erupts ahead —
a silver plashing. Fish with bull heads live below,
with faces like spears, fleshy whiskers, creatures
at home in the channel's clouds of silt and sand.
A towboat approaches, the barge loads of coal:
everything in the river tunes to its blunt power,
must avoid its propeller, its weight, momentum.

I gain on a lily pad broken loose and beside it
a mouse — pale belly up — no longer resisting
the *forward*, the careless and incessant forward.

Past the island, the towboat gone, the wide water
to myself, I rest the paddle, let drift — coast freely.
I am in no-man's-land, far from either side now.
Carefully I lean to scoop up an escaping handful:
it is tepid, cloudy, and original. The potent odor
says everything but you is dissolved in this mix.
I float on its silence, with its anonymous passing.
Current that will bulldoze a stout barn, invade
a town, turns the prow gently this way and that.

Owl

My first night in the country house
October cold set in. I lay exhausted
and slept amid boxes and clutter.
I had moved miles from the town,
left neighbors behind and street light.
An owl's assertion suddenly woke me —
in one of the yard trees nearby:
low vacant calls, random, repetitious.

It was back the same time the second night:
a great horned owl — I learned later —
its head-tearing beak between yellow eyes.
I tossed in bed, pillowed my ears,
gave in finally and began to listen.
It repeated the five-notes *who-ha-who…
whooo-whooo* in erratic intervals.
I heard no progress one call to the next.
At some point, it left off: had made
itself clear, made itself known, I supposed,
flew to the business of the hunt.

And again, the next night. I paid attention.
Each call was a complete message,
each was as it were the first and last.

The first three notes were staccato,
a pause, then the last two — prolonged —
balanced them, resolved the tension.
Each was an utterance, not a speaking,
an announcement, but of what?
If it was I-own-where-we-are,
for a moment I heard more:
its call and the silence before
and after it were of a piece.

An Indian summer night followed.
Darkness was earlier now.
I sank to sleep in balmy quietness.
It was missing, gone:
I was never that close again.

Underneath

A ridge-top farmhouse above creek-bottom fields,
it had been abandoned to the weather for years.
Carpenters still worked as I moved in; they spoke of
the savvy of elder does, personalities of pond fish.
Snakes had nested in the big maple's broken trunk.
Beneath the run-down house, coyote and hedge hog
had shared shelter. Ever heard of such, a roofer asked.
Scat of quick-waddling hog and coyote littered
the leaf-strewn parlor that became my study —
a west room of afternoon sun, last autumn warmth.

I walked the place summer and fall and fit well in it.
Months pass and one day, looking up from the desk,
you find the house is as much within you as out.
Joints ticked on cold nights, the chimney fluted wind.
A length of king snake slid under the wooden porch.
Field mice issued from the heating vents—and spiders.
One evening I heard gnawing on, was it a floor joist?
Those below heard my life transposed to another key:
the pine floor's stressed *chirking* beneath my steps,
the piped flushings, sudden thump of a dropped book,
first, soft morning tread, sudden run for the phone —
the late night fall and laugh of the drunken one above.

At the Window

The wind had worked all morning
then the noise—thud—startled me.
A stout limb landed upright, pitched
and leaned against the study window.
I seized up and shuddered in the belly:
large enough, it could have killed.
Stopped just feet from my quiet desk,
a dead limb from the maple overhead.
A reversal held for a long moment:
I existed in the limb's world—
it was not subject to mine.
It stood propped against the window
thick, leafless, gray, and I left it
a while to indicate where I live.

In the Orchard

The apples are ripe. Down the long rows
they hang above the uncut orchard grass.
The owner is ill. An old man I care for,
of another time, he's with his doctors.
He's in a white bed thinking of his life
when he can. Limbs weigh the red apples,
each fruit with its own earth-roundness.
But I need to mow — came here to work.

I have keys to the stale house, the barn.
There's a foul odor under the porch.
The rusty bush-hog's axle is cracked,
and I'm to bring some order here.
I bloody my thumb with the drill,
lie in the tall grass and get back up.
The fall sun is hot. The sun simply *is*, is.
Slipping off my hat, I bask for a while,
lean on the ladder leaning on a tree.
I pull a red apple down — a plump one
that is streaked with auroral color.
The tough stem, the thin link, is dry.
The first bite — chunk — breaks clean:
it is firm and watery, sweet as cola,
and now I let my hoarded breath go.

The Blue-Tailed Skink

October nights cool, and it absents
the front porch and by an obscure path
passes beneath the house to the back
steps that warm by late morning.
I too am drawn there by the sun.
If we do not see the same house,
I want to say there is only one.
The lizard is silent as the stone
and boards are. I move finally,
cannot help but tower over it.
And it's gone: the uncanny blue—
neon-bright—vivid in after-sight.
I would, yet I cannot protect it.
It is wise to run, should, must,
but if there is not one house,
neither I think are there two.

Winter on the Cumberland

The kayak runs aground on sandbar
beneath a foot of cloudy, cold water.
I climb out in high boots and pull it
by its line to the edge where the river—
a dark-green—abruptly deepens again.
The water's wide here at the mouth.
The kayak drifts quickly from me—
the nylon cord stretches taut.
Insistent current tugs away at the line
like a thief all but strong enough.
You learn exactly how irresistible
river is if you have to swim it.
Flesh takes its temperature. The boat,
my sliver—now I draw it back to me.

Gulls in Winter Light

Brilliant noon light on the colorless river
streams and dazzles as if it were spring.
One gull inspects the fish, a mud-colored carp
lying in algae at the frigid water's edge.
The other birds look on and look away,
a fretful chorus of twenty or so.
The large bird probes a gill slit delicately with its beak
and soon eats an opening its head can fit in.
A few sly birds stand near enough to threaten
but contain themselves. They peck instead
at the bonelike driftwood and nothing.

Suddenly a clucking child outruns his mother
and lunges at the birds that quickly scatter
but are undaunted. They watch as she gathers up
the child in her fur coat. He's deposited still cooing
in the stroller, and the gulls loosely reassemble
and walk on webbed feet back to the precious fish.
The big bird resumes its work on the entrails
that warmed as the water warmed in May.
The fish's stiffened mouth does not object.
Its fins jut like an odd attempt at wings.
Waves wash up in series, and the carcass
flips over as if revived in the moving water.

The bigger bird—wings pumping in bright air—
keens and hovers over it. The waves subsiding,
the fish lies the same. The gull lights on it,
perches on the remnants, then, inexplicably
leaves, yields, flies free, rejoins the pack.
For a moment, silence. The river's faint rustling.
All the gulls converge on the cold flesh at once
raising a nasal cry, unbearable if it were human.

The Backyard, Late Winter

Under glittering snow: last year's grass, and beneath
its dormant roots, the burrows of the chipmunks.
Crusted snow covers the mouth of their tunnels.
Their bold stripes do not signify in that blackness.
Such sleepers, they may be half-eaten before waking.
I wake suddenly myself, anxious, and doze off again.
They're absorbed fully in earth household's silence.
Wind rattles ice-stiff limbs—they hear nothing of it
yet in a darkness beyond porch light and moonlight
perhaps they know, as through an opaque curtain,
a delicate pleasure: they tilt toward a return and
again the world where a giant sun comes and goes.

Raking in Late March

Brown oak leaves knee-deep along the fence
cover mice nests, loose fur, scat,
and revealed here a small opening
in the earth: an entrance
to a vein of pure darkness.

*

Erratic winds sweep away
the raked leaves
and unraked. They whirl off
the biggest pile — released
into the wild again.
I too am here
to interrupt and remove.

*

A honeysuckle runner sprouted
beneath the broken leaves:
white leaflets scrolling a white vine
like a sordid human thing come to light.
Take the cool sun now.

*

Paper-thin leaves are the currency
of a failed state. Inflation doubles
every day. The wheelbarrow full
of leaves, you wait in line.
They will buy you one —
count it — loaf of stale bread.

    *

Winds high-up speed a lone cloud
straight at the sun: eclipse.
The feeling of winter revives
for a minute — the last freeze.
I didn't know it was in me.
Now it's god-bright again.

    *

Exposed, something orange and finger-thick
retreats beneath the leaf bag.
It's a hundred-legged — very fast,
poison-tipped, I think, untouchable.
A creature of the underside —
the immemorial foundation,
it's not itself in the sun.

At Home, Sick, But Feeling Better

    My car resembles a rocket—
        a handsome ship thinking
always and only straight ahead,
        yet each day in the driveway
it has grown more inert.
        Sparrows peck around it
for what in the thin red gravel?
        One perches on a door handle.
One flits under the front end
        to die there at high speed
then at the rear flies up the air.
        The birds, in a former life
Chinese acrobats, lift off—jet
        toward a newly turned field.
The April sun is stronger now
        than any memory of winter.
The white car, that neither
        intends nor does not intend
to kill everything in its path,
        stands in the morning sun, is
warmed and dumbly shines.

At Lusk Creek Canyon

A moment before it was a fallen limb
to step over then suddenly beneath
our feet a snake
lay irrefutable across the trail.
The dark-red, hour-glass bands of copperhead:
a snake, alert, snake-thick,
naked to the light.
One second, I felt I might pour through the air
into the lidless eyes of it—
the next, I would rock
smash the menace from it.

The arrow point of the head lifts—
suspends itself mid-air and cocks
as the rest of it slides
along itself into the ancient coil.
The red tongue lets go toward us three times
then nothing. The blank stare
is at us—and everywhere—at once.
It does not move; it knows how still
a root lies half-buried.
Without words I think:
it always knows what to do
even if that is to die.

My voice returned then: let us live, let it.
I uttered a sharp sound that said
I respect you but I am strong too,
and I stamped once. It disappeared quickly
into the dense mesh of dead grass:
the clean, firm muscle of it, the certainty.

Then the trail was empty before us,
the moist trail
in weak sun near noon.
I stood with her in the cool April air.
We were stopped on a ridge
among broom sedge and stunted cedars.
The light was tenuous and thin —
any moment the wind might sweep it
away down the canyon steeps.

Open Secret

At Ten Years Old

It was a place where two small creek canyons met,
a green hollow shadowed and bright by turns.
One bank was thicketed — vines tangled it.
Another was red, earthen, soft — giving way.
The iron aroma of wet rock was strong.
The quietness here was busy with itself and not
an absence of us and our voices.
A tree's pale contorted roots were exposed
washed bare by the stream. A crawfish, silently intent,
walked its many-legged walk into a deeper pool.
There were snakes here, they said, as if I were at fault.
A spider crossed the water's sky-blue skin.
You could drown, they said. Don't go alone.

I returned in all weathers, unpredictably,
back to linger and without purpose to explore.
The two streams skimmed with white ice in winter
except for the water's rustling v where they joined.
From the snowy rim, I looked down into this
open yet secret, earth-walled place.
It was itself: it continued, sharply, coldly itself,
yet seemed to recall and know me.

A spring rise receded. It left the lowest sandy bank
encrusted with leaf flakes, a claw, acorns,
drowned feathers, grounds on the way
back to the maternal void. I squatted there
and gazed about: new green was inching up
between the stones. Odors, chaste and fetid,
roused in the sun. A snake-skin hung in cattails.
Mud sucked at my shoes. Dragon flies scanned me.
I waded, crawled, upended things, sat, inspected
and sometimes, for a moment sensed my presence.
I was visible, palpable, a force separate
from the place, small, yet might dent it, disrupt—
all the while it grew and lodged in me.

The Ohio at Smithland

Locked and dammed, it's still too large to be contained,
too far across — beyond human scale. One can't hold
both sides in mind at once. It is not the river Thames
or Seine: it dwarfs the traffic of barges a block long.
There's no floodwall here. Stories of floods pass down
like biblical epic. Meandering shoreline is often steep
or crumbling or thicketed and odorous. No graceful
approach or park beckons since the swift spring rise
will foot by foot gain back all but the levee ground.
The busy town drives past. A young couple spreads
a blanket bankside for an hour, but this is to study each
other in its immense light. A suicide's car, still running,
is found one morning abandoned where she waded in.
Adulterers park: their urgent hands, rapt face-to-face.
Midnight, boys gun their loud trucks on the boat ramp —
a beer can clatters down the stone rip-rap, headlights
rake over the dark water. Pittsburgh, Wheeling, Louisville:
the factories' feverish shit clouds it, farm toxin runoff.
The poor work perilous tows and dredges, take its smells
home, are privy to what the others feel beneath them.
Year after year, deckhands drown, drunken fisherman.
What lives in and on it survives if at all in spite of us.

Northern gulls retreat here to winter, then manic bank swallows summering. The hungry birds circle over it and dive — mirroring shadowy fish that rise to feed. Near in, a rippling — a small snake surfaces, carefully tastes the air. Only the tall blue heron, all but invisible, stands gazing in the shallows as if it were immune.

A World

1. *The Farm*

Five ponds dot the farm — various shapes and ages.
All brim with chill spring rain. From above they look
like small islands of light. Across a gusting surface,
sky ripples and fades, appears, and is swept away
like days lasting seconds. A heron sails down,
lands at the pond nearest the house, wades in.
A great blue, it's poised, looks self-absorbed,
yet if I appear at the door it instantly lifts away.

The bird steps in deeper and pauses with one foot —
the twiglike toes — held mid-air, the other spreads
wide in the algaed muck. Now the wind falls off.
In the vast above, it can hear the mosquito din
of a jet; one pond over the jawking of kingfisher.
It sights down the spearhead of its beak with the
empty eyes of the present. Each peaking instant
just before it arrives must gather all of the past.
A stout fish, a striking orange bluegill rises
effortlessly now in the murk, glints with light
and as if signaled, with a deft flicker vanishes.
The heron's statue is neither more still nor less.

11. *At School*

A jet crosses the blue vacuum above the campus.
Sequestered as we are indoors we don't hear it.
I wait before my students in the strained silence.
They sit at their desks in the chaste classroom:
freshmen, intent, poker-faced. We've just met.
The cogent question I've asked can't please them.
Above the fluorescent ceiling, there's a whistling
inhalation of air as a door opens elsewhere, closes.
A slender girl dressed as irredeemable rock star
studies the radiance of the tall curtained window.
Leaning lightly on my desk, I broadcast a smile.
There's too much I want to tell — reveal to them.
They guard new souls. Is it captivity they resist?
I admire the vigorous hair, the hip's lean wedge,
fruitlike breasts. They're self-conscious, tentative,
yet the loveliness never stutters. But it's time.
I address those in back and zero in: 'Students
sometimes say they think it's true — and you?'

Flood

Rain pours down day into night — dense rain green
with April's leafing out, sheets of drowning rain,
valley-long storms. Mud-red creeks race and surge.
The river spreads inch by inch half a mile across
its floodplain. It sucks at weeds and at new gardens.
The current plucks away fence posts, slender willows.
It drafts our thoughts to it, hauls away winter trash.
Flushed out snakes slide into barns, under porches.
A child at Cypress has drowned, a diver after him.
I cross my sodden yard again to the sandbag wall:
it hemorrhages river. The chill brown water laps
near the top. Now a propane tank — a silver bomb —
casually drifts into view. A raft of foam and litter
comes from one nowhere on the way to another.
The current draws one into mindless fascination:
it may seem to have agency — an ominous intent,
yet it can do nothing of course but what it does.

I lie in bed awake, imagine the cabin under water:
murky kitchen window implodes, clothes swim
out of closets, books levitate and open their wings.
Dozing off, I dream the place lifts like a houseboat
and bears me away. It speeds downstream, it tilts
left and right, water in one corner then another —
floor a sinking deck. I skirt an islanded hilltop,

black cows left stranded on it. Their idiotic faces
turn to me, bawling and pleading as I sail past.

At dawn we check the high-heaped wall again:
the sandbags seep river, spurt river. A bitter man
at Cairo dynamites his own town's levee. It's time:
in two hurried loads I remove my dearest things.
Atop the steep cemetery hill, I park and take it in:
green river presses at the side of the hive-like town.
There are news vans, the Guard trucks, the tourists,
police, and children biking — festive — in the streets.
The Cumberland's mouth widens to the west where
the two rivers — uncontainable — join in the fields.
They mingle their shadowy green and milky brown,
slack off in waist-high backwaters, impromptu lakes.
The island's submerged, only green treetops show:
tugged under a long moment, up they spring again.
My campsite's underwater, the trails, burrows filled.
All that could, swam. The vast floodplain shimmers,
is fluid with light. The cool rivers are at large and
West now: horizon-wide, blue-dark clouds sail to us
in ranks oddly uniform and stately. East: it's rain in
the mountains — and south to Nashville, heavy rain.
One can lose it all, I think, release it all: let it go.

June Rain

Her place was pocketed in woods,
and we came out the backdoor without pause
naked from the bed we had done
the best we could to overturn—
out into a light summer rain.

It was an in-between time
before her crisis—inner and financial.
How to content myself I couldn't say.
Not knowing what we needed,
we did not look ahead or look away.

I pulled her down in soaking grass.
We'd found the combination: a kiss
that opened doors from head to toe.
Little twigs and ants clung to us.
Desire worked to persuade us
we are gods and at last succeeded.
We believed, but one cannot grasp
even this once and for all.

The sky at one point cleared above the trees
still the rain fell, and sunlight
glittered in the headlong drops.

We were sopping—slick with it
yet afterward found our knees, elbows
red from the firm ground.

Summer Midnight

The moon was full and the yard luminous.
It was like a shadow day loud with
the body music of frogs and cicadas.
The monotony of the voices came to soothe.
Just across the threshold from their desire
I lay sleeping, was slowly breathed by sleep:
a benign emptiness drew me in for long moments
then released me, once and for all it must be.
Suddenly I sat up, was sitting up:
a yodeled cry climbed the scale of pain
and — quickly cut off — fell away.
Something — it was surely wild —
was killed in the creek bottom.
In its scream, brief — a moment —
I heard it resist, suffer wholly,
not ask why, see the end opening,
spring through it and go.

I stood in the dark on the back porch steps.
The moon was gone but the night still busy:
crickets, frogs, and the others uninterrupted
were ratcheting and seducing and trilling.
The one I'd heard had no doubt preyed to live itself,
had hunted in that same fatal field.
Ice water I poured down ached in my teeth.

The bedroom window closed, I lay down again.
I hovered in the trance before sleep,
and the shadowed farm, the fields and woods—
this place within me, with me in it, began to
compose itself again: leaf by beatific leaf,
the mouths that eat and sing, the silent ground.

Meeting after Weeks of Separation

We parked separately on the ramp beside the river.
The early summer night was warm, permissive,
and she came — eagerly it seemed — to my car to sit.
I kissed her, but see now it was merely allowed.
The taste of her was unchanged: a moistness
somehow chaste, a flavor smoky and clean.
We could hear through the open windows
the rustling and lapping of the river water.
We had two hours, she said. Absurd to think
hours, to put it thus, what I might say or do
to move close to her again. The mechanism
that was in place — in charge, instead of us,
might take days to uncover and name, defuse.

I'd brought good wine. We made sly comedy
when we drank. We'd go on privately smiling
when others around us were inanely serious.
We sipped and talked. I thought, let it meander.
She revived an old complaint, but checked herself.
Cool air and odor rose off the river's dim body.
We should speak of the obvious, our failure:
each approach I found it overgrown, snake-held.
It lay in us both and neither, in the combination,
couldn't be reduced: the problem was ourselves.

A car beating with country music cruised past,
some commonplace of pathos and resignation.
We sat in the emptiness of an ordinary moment.
I embraced her, carefully, and she shrank away.
What I said next — barbed, flip, sank in silence.
The sun-roof above us framed a patch of sky
with its stars in their fixed and random order.
She began to steer us toward unearned harmony.
And I was a crank if I resisted. I did not resist.
Then it was time: her other life, the only one,
waited on her. She unfolded an errand list as if
in evidence, her looped handwriting like a girl's.
It was a false good-bye as if we'd meet again.
She walked to the familiar car. I ridiculed it
to myself: its subtle ostentation. I didn't wave.
She drove off slowly — tentatively? A future
of course can only accrete — inhabited, enacted.
I turned on the headlights, switched them off.
We'd met here often. For weeks I would avoid it.
Summer and fall were full of everything but her:
I went on faulting her, desiring, forgiving nothing.

Trail

I.

Our restless Boone follows the trail
under the canopy of old growth,
treks through its branching shadows
then out into grassland, going where?
He camps near the buffalo trace
we will pave later as the highway
that shoppers take to the new mall.
It's lit up in the dusk for its opening.
It might be a cruise liner docked at
the edge of a vast, dim cornfield.
A spotlight reaches sky it seems.
Families and boys and girls stroll
the wide, musicked corridors where
no past intrudes, future, time of day.

II.

Animals use this vague gravel lane
near the mouth of the Cumberland:
the wild turkeys process, rabbits fly,
the coyote zigzags, nose-to-ground.
The slow cars of lovers come and go
at night: headlights, windows down,
red tip of cigarette. Exiting the lane,
they take the levee road, cruise past:
rap beat of the speakers thumping.

Follow it, the grassy lane plays out
in a clearing that saplings and weeds
have taken back. They cover over
the mossed bricks of a foundation.
Yellow jonquils light up in spring.
Pale mushroom-like condoms lie
among the forbs. At the far end of
the clearing a deer path threads its
subtle way into the woods, second
growth or third. The summer leaves
that waver in green air have, limb
on limb, begun to shut out the sky.

The Wife

The young wife, offended, ran a cool scented bath,
ready for a self-absorbed soaking. The gardener,
overheated, hung-over, weeded in a stifling bed.
The storm approached, hushing and darkening.
Now the house takes the rain's blind thrashing —
erratic winds fling it against the tall windows.
In the half-lit green world out back, the big tree
is pressed upon, leans, and suddenly uproots
and goes down, its root-tangle up-rearing.
They — wife and husband — should stand clear
of the fragile window but are riveted there.
A horse — a rain-sheeted horse appears, runs
the drive past the trellised side-porch with head
held rigidly high as if to avoid the confusion
into which it disappears, the wind's wild spray.
A sorrel mare, she noticed, with a white sock.
The sash loose, her silk robe hangs half-open.
Two socks, he says, and feigns an arm blow.

She walks out in the odd quiet of late afternoon —
the young wife who wants to be unfaithful and
cannot. A tall girl, she is athletic and animated
and when she frowns she resembles her mother
who moved away, rarely calls. Summer's hit song
floats through her — a slow surrender, dreamy
yet with the urgency of the blues. She'd like
a job — to find more in herself, and he says no.
She pauses beside the disheveled grape arbor.
He is a pig in bed, all thrust and then nothing.
Past the stone barn, she sees the downed tree,
the huge sycamore. It has been tall as long as
anyone, the oldest neighbors, can remember.
Now its stout branches are broken beneath it.
Half of it lies across the smaller, deeper pond —
its white limbs penetrate the dim, green water.
Pale fish already swim among the dense leaves,
nose and prod them. They are bold as fingers
yet turn quickly to the cool darkness and dive.

Turkey Vultures

Summer thermals rise above the ridge farm
where the vultures often float in meditation
high enough one can't see the head's red flesh.
Five or six of them cruise vaguely together:
a high, slow hanging, effortless veer and sway.
One suddenly begins its long balletic glide
down to earth's warm body. Others follow
as if down a chute out of the clean blue sky.
I look the next day, and they're up again.
Whose eyes know the ridge as well, inch by
green inch? — the rain-washed backs of
all on four legs, chaste bright tops of heads,
my meandering walks — vivid expeditions
from which I bring back all I can alive.

Watery Days

In my cabin at the mouth of the Cumberland
windows face both rivers: a place of watery days
and flowing light, gulls aloft, algae's green odor.
I wake in the night: a spot-lit towboat tunnels
the blackness in studied slow-motion. I sleep:
vague first light is verified on the naked flats.
I'm at the desk for hours through the morning,
the flicker of river in the corner of my eye.
In minutes I can be out on the live, wide water:
its restless and silent arriving…*here is as now is.*

January is rain-soaked: days of ashen light, sleet
chasing rain. The river swells, it's smoking-cold.
The flood in May: water moving water. It eddies,
it swallows, and canoeing it is reckless, ecstatic.
July afternoons: white light on it scalds the eyes.
In blanched September, the river lags, recedes.
It drops slowly down its steep, musty banks.
The water wafts the odor of a rich, foul stew.
Long sandbars emerge and on them evidence
of what swam below lies baking in the sun:
white fish bones, a turtle shell is an empty box.
I beach the canoe on a strip narrow as sidewalk.
The glaring water slides past me on either side.

To stand in its midst: this is what I wanted.
It can't be surveyed or grid-lined or owned.
In the hot sand, like hieroglyphs, footprints
of a blue heron end where it leapt airborne.

October morning: the windows white with fog.
The river runs beneath it: a secret, rustling water
one can only imagine, river intimate with itself.
November: geese high on their fly-way South—
the v's faint, too far gone in my photograph,
the unswerving calls lost in the blue distance.
Christmas, a journal's filled: notes on weather,
the season's and the sky-bearing river's moods.
It reads like one's hidden life, a diary in code.
New Year's Day: the Ohio is millennia old.
Night rain goes on all morning with intent:
dimly-lit, the river's up, rising, flushing clean.

A Meaningless Creek Pebble

I toss it among the countless others
in the dry gravel of the creek bed.
It is small as a pea, smooth, cool
to touch, the red color of iron
at earth's immense molten core.
Blood too is red with it, one's blood.

The Roof

Days pass, why would I think of it:
the cabin's roof peaking overhead,
there unseen as I work and sleep,
starlight on it subtle, enigmatic.

    *

The sudden battering above
is torrential rain, rain of a chill
January night, a black waterfall.
I lie blanketed and immune:
it's thrilling—the roof's coarse,
impervious hide is enough.
Ladder up, next day I inspect it:
the shingles are worn and bare
and some loose, others buckling.

    *

Late September, dry, the river's low.
I launch the kayak and am soon
downstream. I glance back:
the cabin's quickly receding.
It's all but out of sight:
a point the cool light falls on.
It's exposed always. The earth
itself is: bare at every moment.
The sky's a purest lucent blue.

Burred, Mute Stray Dog

The black stray is in the yard again.
He lies in the parched grass as I drive up.
He's at ease in the shining fall air.
To gnaw on this time he has brought
a deer shin with its cloven hoof.
I shout: he leaps up, his head bobs,
the whole body equivocates, yet he retreats
only so far, staring back over his shoulder.
He's young or ungrown, dingy black.
The unoffendable snout lingers
where I peed beside the hedge.
What he senses I think he knows absolutely.

'Go on now.' I fling gravel, 'Go!'
He runs. He's covering his rear with his eyes.
He's down the bank for a drink of green river.
I'm in a porch chair when he returns.
In the drive he turns to face me
slack-jawed. The pink tongue lolls forth
over stout yellow teeth. He's lupine
but he avails himself— offers it seems
all he is for a hand-out, an embrace.
He would never leave, I know it.
'Go.' I shout. 'Don't ask me why, *go.*'

Fleeing, he stops in a patch of golden rod.
He observes me. 'Nothing's final,'
the buoyant tail says, 'Gods can change
their minds in an instant. I've seen it.'
Front, then back legs scratch up dust,
a cloud that quickly envelopes him.
He has nothing to do but know
what he can of the earth. He has time.
And I resist him: I have to.

Mandala

The small spider, weightless,
in some way fearless, surely,
lowers itself through the air.
Midway it stops — hesitates,
assesses — then hurtles down
to the rug beside my desk.
I lose it in the design of
woven flowers and leaves.

All summer, spiders stitched
corners of the house together —
tiny ones and large, elusive,
and I vacuumed them away.
Yesterday one stretched its
life and death mandala across
a pane of the south window
where September light pours in.

There's the glint beside me now
of a loose strand hanging in air.
The slightest stir and light runs
along it, streaks instantaneously
up and down it — here and gone —
subtlest interworking of the day.

Quick Red Squirrel Cartoon

Acorns sail down from the high
branches of the great oak,
and the hawk will also.
A plump acorn: the squirrel
eats it or buries it — plants
it beneath the dry grass.
Its front paws are hands
to feed its little teeth
machine, and when it runs
the paws again are feet.
The acorn may vanish in
the squirrel, or in the earth —
the hawk watches it might
be from another world.

Each of the squirrel's acts
seems tentative yet isn't
felt so, surely, or all
its life is provisional.
A mild fall breeze stirs:
air is the hawk's medium.
The squirrel twitches its
head right, back, left.
Its sentence: it cannot
read all omens at once.

A manic sprint saves it
as in a child's cartoon.
The hawk sails off, retires
it could be, then without
arriving appears again
on the muscular gray limb
above our roofs and ladders.

Out of the Half World

I.

The cool stars as if of no consequence fade,
and the owl with the feathered horns rests
with the kill inside him.
The river is still, black, a great seam of coal.
At riverside, in high cottonwood dark,
the owl utters himself in what once
were words, purified now
of ambiguity, of abstraction.
Lucid sleeper, a rabbit wakes
to the calls, eyes up, around,
and looks to the East — the void
most susceptible to the light.

II.

Mounds of darkness above the river
resolve slowly into rounded hills
dappled with what must be houses.
The yard trees that surround them
remain obscure, self-absorbed.
The dove notes begin to rise and fall:
to the sleepless, they say understanding
is only in pained aftermath.
Buried in bed, I want none of it.

During the long moment
before waking, I'm gazing back
into the half world, savoring
a lawless dream.

   III.

The October sun emerges:
a pale orange sun — cool, foreign,
uncalled for it seems.
A tan moth worn out
by the porch light flutters down.
The skink slips from the cleavage
in the cabin's weathered foundation.
He gazes into the light, but takes
to himself only the smallest glints —
the sliver of his icy blue tail.

A stillness pulsing, pulsing, he reads
the odors of the air where everything
dead and living combine.
An instant away is a wasp the night
chill has slowed to a crawl.

Each of the lizard's four limbs, as in a test,
takes a turn and moves him forward
an inch to the edge
of the day.

   IV.

I swipe the steamy bathroom window,
gaze out slack-eyed. The cabin's shadow
is a remnant block of night.
Along its edge, robins browse
a bright patch of grass
as if light were edible.
Two loud jays rake the pale air.
I leap ahead to work, to class, and miss
a moment here as it's added
to the revelation morning is.
Purposes and uses spread quickly
from one room to the next.
The phone rings, and — jarred — I let it.
The voice of the teacher in me
begins tuning up, calling for attention.

Searching for the keys, I kneel
by the bed and look under:
they glimmer in the twilight.
The last dream draws me back:
the shadow woman who sensed
my desire before I did.
I think hold to it, carry it —
a talisman — into the day.

    v.

Breakfast goes down. I switch off lamps.
Near the kitchen window, a flashing red
cardinal takes charge of the yew bush.
Light clarifies the air. A palest gold,
it occupies the wide flats of the river.
The cardinal — chit…*chit chit chit* —
chips away bright flecks of sound
until like a bear with briefcase
swinging I burst from the back door.
A creature masked for performance
among humans, I go quickly down
the steps and to the car — into time.

On a Walk to the Supermarket

Thousands of birds aloft — a whirring throng of starlings
sweep over me, a fretful black cloud that fills the sky.
They descend suddenly en masse — voices croaking —
and fill a host of trees, the great oaks empty of leaves.
Modest houses line the street and ordinary parked cars.
Up some birds swarm again inexplicably and swirl
away in the air then reverse field and spill down
lighting on roofs, in yards. Stragglers jostle, contest
for perches head to tail — bristle and drop paste.
They have no nest, no baggage. Are seeking food?
They work their beaks, it might be making words.
The shrill chaos of voices is no music but it joins
each to the whole — and if not in ecstasy, it surely
amplifies desire and need and will in every one.

The afternoon's upended, November cold forgotten.
Doors are opening, windows not cracked for weeks.
People stand confused on doorsteps and walkways:
they're fascinated and alarmed and like me repulsed.
They curse, wave arms. The colony ignores them.
The birds will roost for the night is it, the winter?
The citizens will not allow this in their tidy yards,
on their mortgaged roofs. They throw gravel now,
fling acorns, sticks, beat tin pots, weirdly hooting.

No Help

By late fall: few spiders, yet webs remain.
Lines anchor a fern frond to the desk.
Each day lady bugs appear. On the red dome,
the painterly touch of the black spots.
They careen through the warm oasis of the house.
Their eject on the fingers is dryly bitter.

One has caught in window sill strands
and struggling, further enchains itself.
Tiny oar-like legs row in the air.
Like origami folded in on itself, the wings
emerge from under the hinged shell.
They too entangle. The creature
is intermittently motionless
then at work on its predicament again.
Glacial noon light fills the window.

Minutes rise to the ceiling where the warmth is
and slowly coalesce into an hour
then another. No help arrives, nor is there
a sudden advance along the rigging,
no bite like a stab of sleep.
But then it bumbles free.

The Deer of Seven Mile Creek

Mid-December: they are in rut and hunted.
In the bleak first light and the dusk light
the trails they must walk may be fatal.
Does, fierce matriarchs, shepherd fawns
along paths that meander the bare woods,
the slender does whose hoof-strikes kill.
The does' scent and the waning light sets
the bucks off — necks swollen, they spray
piss, shred saplings — ozone snorting bucks
that were loners until now. They pitch one
against the other, antler to antler, fuming,
as if to banish all others like themselves.
A stout one steps high and openly as a lion
across the green of a winter wheat field.

He will stalk her without relief for a week —
she with perhaps one day and night in heat.
Can they see each other glow, as we do
sometimes when the other opens to us.
Soon the antlers and god's power fall away.
Does seclude themselves in winter yards.
Their black eyes narrow in the blown snow.
The long back mantles with downy flakes,
and it swells within her warm underbelly:
the blood form and dim dream of fawn.

Death of a Mouse

He has dragged the trap into the open
and is exposed on the shiny kitchen floor.
The bar wedged deep in his lower back.
Dead, I think, dead, I hope,
but as I lift the trap the pink paws dig
in the air, and I quickly drop it.
He lies still. Many long moments
I peer closely: once he slowly blinks.
The delicate funnel of ear, rapid breaths
caving in his sides, the limp tail.
In the black eyes: nothing for me.
I must finish him — and resent it.

I hold the trap from me in the night air.
A can of water sits on the porch rail —
winter rain in a coffee can, deep enough.
The first time his head will not stay under I curse.
He, I realize later, is silent through it all.
He's anchored in frigid water yet his snout
thrusts back up. I'm infuriated.
A fir strip lies on the porch floor beside me —
a flimsy strip he dodges, ducks from under.
I catch the toppling can and strike again
and still the snout emerges up, up
into the ocean of air. I jab until I have it:
yellow porch light lies smooth on the water.

It is dark—overcast—in the back yard.
To release him I have to shake him
loose from the embedded bar.
Cold drops splash my pants.
He falls somewhere in the sharp stubble
beneath the sycamore's high limbs.
I've heard an owl here in the early morning:
the voice of a barn owl—
no violence in it, no reflection.

Crows

Crows perch atop the parking lot lamp-posts.
The five big birds. They're assured, deliberate.
Cah-cah — their voices sound cold, mocking
above the neat rows of the students' cars.
In the deft, black beak of one a white napkin
is lip-sticked or ketchup-stained. One drops to
a hood, peers in the window, another lands
among french fries scattered about like fingers
on the asphalt. A door slams — they all lift off.
They nest in thick woods near the campus.
Their feet are black, the beak and eyes black —
pure essence of crow, all color burnt away.

Cah-cah…the big birds gather in air now
and scouting cruise the frozen ball field.
Four boys in a posse, lean freshmen, cross
the vacant quadrangle. They advance in
pecking order: together, yet each alone.
Punches pulled and threats amuse them.
They're bright, bored, nod asleep in class.
And one night late, the four will linger
in the red neon aura of a roadside club.
Shining bodies of cars will surround them.

The new truck's there: the owner and friends
once shamed them. With knives they line
a door, the hood. They cut wire, slit tires.
And peel off then, panicky, spurting gravel.
In farm country—on a curve they'd know,
their jeep, the paper said, had left the road.
Their leader, I'd taught him, died of burns.

The crows' marriage to the place is absolute—
no segregation of an earth, heaven and hell.
A catch of blood in the air alerts the birds.
There are familial ties; the food hunt binds
them together—and nights the ice welds
itself to the dense branches of their spruce.
Near their nests a gray, vine-ridden barn
stands in a vague clearing and leading to it
a trace of wagon road that is overgrown.
There's the constant roar of the Interstate
in the near distance. They are aware surely
of the road's shrill monotony night and day.

February Cold Front

Afternoon turns colder, grayer.
   The wind going nowhere
whips this way and that across
   the backyard, and the leaves
loose on the ground obey.
   The sparrows could not race
faster—quickly gone, they're
   back now the other way
against the wind as if uphill.
   They wheel and pour down
and light on the woodpile—
   each bird on his own feet.
The split logs were at one
   time a beech tree, and on its
limbs ancestors of the birds
   once chirruped and shat.
Old leaves flung up again are
   clumsily shuffled, halt mid-air,
fall again in disorder—lie in
   another order, perfect and new.
The birds pry up dry bark with
   their beaks. One finds something
edible, a bite; another: nothing,
   and the mind, an artist, probes
beneath its own stale habits
   for blood, for some renewal.

A Vole in the March Snow

A meadow vole digs out of the foot-deep snow.
Up from his tunnel beneath the frozen grasses,
he clambers into the blazing light of morning.
He is small and jittery, his fur shadowy brown.
The porch eaves release drops of snow-melt:
nothing else moves. The vole peers down his
new tunnel, *so…thus,* glances once toward me
then scurries away across the week-old snow
that is slowly sinking. He leaps footprints of
coyote, each a blue void in the shining crust.
I wrap my sweater close and face to the sun.
Melt drops hang then flare mid-air as they fall.
On the bright sky, a careful shape — marsh hawk —
clears the near ridge and descends. The wings
spread and subtly shift as if they too can see.
The vole runs now — it can't be — to the hawk,
and the catch on the fly seems casual, gentle.

In the Rockies

On the high ridge, a parking spot —
a great overlook: I pull off the road.
The grit-flecked snow is in retreat.
The breath of winter rises from it:
what was buried in the deep drifts
exposed to a sun bright as summer.
I ignore the sign and wade into it:
a few feet beyond the stone fence
sheer slope plunges down the height.
At the edge, a blue flower is islanded
in snow that has thinned out here —
a small flower, an opening around it
as if it had shrugged off the snow or
its own iota of warmth had melted it.
Exposed this way, we wouldn't last.
A ground-hugging pasqueflower,
leaves and stalk delicately haired.
It sunbathes in persistent wind
at ease: a miniature blue flower that
is a fact of the mountain's body.

Jonquils

Last year's leaves shine in the tan grass —
dry, broken leaves nearer
nothing than to any tree.
High clouds pass over as if
toward some other world.
From within the winter sun,
this one — this sun emerges.
The new light one would say,
yet there is no other kind. And even
if it is gusting, interrupted light,
still it is permission: jonquils bloom.

Unprotected in chill wind, the flowers —
cream-yellow cups — yield,
lean back again and
again and are released.
Flu and fever subdued me
as, below, their bulbs opened
themselves like dark purses.
They rose in the side-yard colony
unnoticed — no need of attention.
I though, as if a lover signaled,
need to give them mine.

The Beast

There was cancer and the bowels
shut down, then the kidneys.
I filled with the waste and
black bile, and the mind went.
I was comatose at the end.
I was it? Where was this I?
The beast outlasted me, endured.
I wrote later *the sturdy beast* —
I pulled rank on my body. It?
He drug me from the putrid field.
I thank him: does he hear me?
He is silent, at work always.
He only speaks through me?
This is his voice is what I say.

After a Near Fatal Illness

It's a day mild enough to recuperate
in the open on the wooden deck.
I lie empty — quiet — on the chaise.
The sun warms the length of me
sensual and chaste. I'd forgotten.
Green softens the lawn and trees.
I can feel myself healing
as if tiny bees — a subtle art —
sealed the wounds from within.
I need weeks to rest, safely enclouded.
Napping, I'm caught suddenly
in nightmare: the hospital, masked faces.
The surgeon cuts me to the quick.

I wake, lying still, in calm sun again.
A breeze plays over me, my robe.
April is real enough: the birds believe it.
A neighbor mows. Others do
what I did, teach the classes —
ease into the vacancies, my roles.
Sun penetrates and warms the air.
Light passes through the pale orange
of my closed eyelids as through
a thin curtain, nothing more.

The Old Mayfield Road

Families on small farms that went
back generations lived there, men in
overalls whose quiet gazes belonged
it seemed to me in another century.
Their wives were tireless, gracious.
My great grandparent's dairy farm
faced that gravel road. Grandfather
took it to town for his weekly gospel
singing, politicking, and romance.
It was later paved, yet few would
drive it if not connected by family
or land to the local past. Rural life:
it was all we had for so long, and in
the fields and meadows we fought
our war against ourselves, let blood.
Jefferson's yeoman farmers: how far
back in American mist they seemed
and yet was this not them here on
the road of my grandfather's birth?
We were in my early years leaving
them behind as fast as we could.

I took the serpentine road myself
sometimes, but kept the car radio
of the present playing. The farms
in corn and milo were well-kept—
green fields on land that softly
swelled and dipped. The work
demanded here was lost on me.
A frame house rode atop a crest,
a silo, a tobacco patch. I slowed
for an unnerving wooden bridge.
A Baptist church, white and plain,
stood at a crossroad and behind it
the benign presence of black cows
meadow-grazing. A sleek hot-rod
by a barn was adorned with hell's
orange flames, at home somehow.
A creek bottom kitchen garden
over ran its neat rows. Tomatoes
hung — blood-red drops — on vines.
The beans' green tendrils topped
their poles, unwound in the light.
I sped on to see a Mayfield girl.

The farm people brought to town
their melons, the hams, tan eggs
washed in cool water from a spring.
The slow voices stood out in town
on Saturday mornings when I was
a boy and my grandfather led me
by the hand among them. If still
like them, he had been elected —
had a mid-town avenue address.
In an even tone like theirs — they
could be raucous too, he would
introduce me, and they were kind.

Trumpet Vines on Shawnee Island

No one has ever lived here, the river prohibits
but trumpet vines spread through the dry cane—
the orange-flowered vines climb anything living
or dead to be nearer the summer sun. The flowers
appeal to the sturdy black bees that like cavers
with legs churning enter the vulval blossoms.
Deer, raccoon and others living here must swim
when the Ohio in swift flood immerses the island.
The hardy vines persist, reach farther every year.
And if all of it, the road-webbed continent were
returned to the tribes? The vines would still grow
if east, the White House were no longer needed—
were carefully dismantled, and each heavy door,
bust and white brick and painting were given to
the uncertain citizens and their eager children.
A vine occupies a bare, unrooted tree that flood
left off. It's climbed up, elegantly around and
up to the highest limb and—above my head—
opened orange flowers lined with a lurid red.

Thunderstorm

Late summer, the scorching, windless afternoons stretch on,
deer flies ruin even a short walk to Island Pond,
everywhere — limp leaves, and the tall weeds bow down.
In the wide creek bottom, dark green corn stands motionless
like a cool lake where the deer might plunge in.
A blue wasp bumps the back door screen, turns and sails
the dim hallway toward the illumined window in front.
The attic fan drones through my nap, a feverish dream,
and a rust-orange moth with eyed-wings hovers
savoring the salty shirt draped on the porch rail.
At 6:00, it feels like noon and all of it baking, baking.
The car seat burns. The lane billows red dust in the rearview.
Slow, believing insects sail into the windshield.
Seven Mile Creek no longer reaches the river and stands
in pools: green and still, skimmed with empty sky.
Rich river odor, vaguely sexual, rises under the long bridge.
Receding water has left terraced shelves down the sandy bank.
Fish browse among cool rails of light in the cloudy channel:
even if they knew it was poisoned, where would they go?

With their backs to the river are weedy truck yards,
a small gay nightclub, the storefront Bethel Tabernacle —
all their windows fogged with fine limestone dust.
An elderly black couple sits and fans on a tottering porch.
In the bare yard, two wee boys kick-box in bathing suits.

It's Sunday: the streets downtown are deserted, the sidewalks
dumb with heat. Stores have closed, windows papered over.
Near the Interstate—in earshot of its shrill, constant stream,
citizens hurry from cool cars in the sprawling parking lot
into movie dark or the dream-world of a million things.
A girl home from college thumbs through underwear
the color of champagne. Her mask broadcasts impatience
with the small town, the stagnant news. It will be years if ever
she sees herself clearly, hidden here in plain sight.
A chorus line of color TVs shows a storm-cloud flotilla
cruising slowly up the serpentine river valley. It will strike
after midnight, but simulated in greens and golds it's seen
in time-lapse now to appear out of nothing, half vanish,
materialize, change shapes like a god stalking an earthly love.

Cold rain hurtling down blurs the pitch-black air now.
Thunder rolls sound like mountain sides collapsing.
A branched lightning shaft stands forth vivid as neon
and strikes a slender tower of the mile-long bridge—
jags down it along a pillar and brands the dark water.
The vast river plain—grain and bean fields—lights up
as if bombs were dropping. The corn's shallow roots
draw water up the stalk on the way to stunted ears.
Crickets cling to the undersides of hail-pelted leaves.
Anarchy shakes the spindly trees on neat suburban lawns.

Lightning strikes a ridge farm: the house hit, cheap veneer
splinters the dark air of her bedroom, wall paper is smoking,
a white, sonic-needle penetrates her ears, and the widow —
bawdy, iron-tough — will no more hear her chickens talk.
Basements are filling; stoplights gutter out; a roof leak
is an open spout; a creek sweeps a judge's dog away.
In a grove of blowing willows near the river, the girl
and boy lie bare in the rumpled bed of his camper,
their pale bodies locked together. The chill rain beats
hungrily on the roof. She — it is the girl from the mall —
is far beyond herself as she intended. Yet he's remote.
They have drunk all they had. The ecstatic connection
has been made, the inner passage. A long, unwanted
childbearing — they cannot know of it — has begun.
As they leave, as they navigate uneven, muddy road,
rain that had tamely tapered off starts to splurge again.
Growing things for miles siphon it, fill with it, soothed.
The river will slowly rise, widen and rush and freshen.

I slept, quietness woke me. And I sit in the cool dark
of the screened porch. A light rain descends steadily
as if for long duration, fine rain, an air-thin distillation.
The sloping yard is lost in its dimness. The storm in
its passing worked out a great imbalance. It relieves
like a verdict that has gratuitously gone one's way.
To the north and east, the theatrics grow fainter.
A truth I've avoided can I think instruct me now.
The distant flashes are like afterthoughts, a survivor
memory.... And lying on the chaise, I sleep again.

Mourning Doves

I.

An early memory: I lean, chin on the sill,
listening to low cooing in the yard.
It seems to be the trees themselves.
Dove calls, and the silence between them
dove silences: the easeful intervals
were a first sense of time.
It is the male voice one hears.
The four unhurried, vibrato notes—
no mourning in them I know now,
no sorrow, but the latest dove
news, eons old.

II.

May, early morning: four doves sail in—
touch down on the lane, substantial suddenly.
The mower scattered seed-heads there.
They investigate, plump and waddling.
They're silent, or, perhaps chuckling inaudibly.
The one apart faces East into the raked orange light,
its feathers a subtle chalk-brown
and tan black-flecked as sand.
The others peck grains off the asphalt,
the road useless to them otherwise.

A car barrels through: school boys severing
bright morning air into future and past.
Its growl is like thunder crammed in a box.
The doves—deliberate, portly on small feet—
have no chance, then out of the instant
after the last possible moment,
they're in a blur airborne.
They climb, wings clapping, and
unperturbed it seems
circle back and land in the empty lane
of the present, where they were.

    III.

The pair's nest, loose thatch of sticks,
they placed high in the side-yard magnolia
above my small study window.
The male flies up and broadcasts
from a bare limb atop the pine.
He flexes his elegant tail with each call:
somewhere in the stillness she listens.
His approach is skittish yet implacable,
her fear subsides or is overridden
and blinking, she surrenders.

They couple with no grip on the other:
the slow strokes of his wings
massage the air, hoist
him close in, closer.

Continents divide, collide, the dove
meditates on the two white eggs
warm and humming beneath her.
She broods these summer nights
the Dipper wheels down the West.
He too in turn covers the eggs
through long days with no names,
rests vacantly upon the world to come.
The featureless expanse of my roof
lies below them, bare to the sun.
June light here and there finds entry
among the tree's dense leaves, filters
down in its shadowy green spaces.
The doves have their being there,
feed the infants a milky regurgitation.
Most do not last the first year.

IV.

September, cooler nights, yet a sheet
suffices, scant, delicious on the skin.
Before I wake, they call an invariable dove
realm into existence:
throat-quavered notes, the uptake
then down, down, the last slightly
fading as if out of breath.
The calls linger like a woman's:
the naked moans of a woman heard
beneath the high window of a hotel.

I rise slowly from the dark below…
Conscious suddenly, I lie listening, meek
in the first, faint light, am incarnated
one more time, stiff-necked, a little dazed
with years and needing more than ever
the presence of doves—and all
else that cannot be appropriated.

Here and There

Near dusk, bank swallows feed over the Ohio.
They rise and plunge above its plodding surface.
They will leave soon — it's late September.
The blue and tan river descends a thousand
miles to the incandescent greens of the Gulf.
Wings smaller than one's hand, they'll swim
the air above it. The tireless horizon at last
is rimmed with misting jungle, and there
they'll continue another — a former — life.
In their tunneled nests at night, can they see
themselves a mile high over burning ocean?

Each night the sun lingers elsewhere longer.
Until the day they depart, the birds engorge,
skim from the swarms of midges that hover
the cooling water. They dissolve in the hazy
orange light, reappear in assent, flip and dive.
Two fly ahead of my kayak, circle and from
behind abruptly pass a few feet overhead.
The two muscle the air — precisely where
now goes — with fierce, paper-thin wings.

North Atlantic Herring

It's clouding over, blustery, late fall.
I'm back from canoeing the Ohio,
manning my capsule of a boat.
I sit in the small lit kitchen
inland seven hundred miles.
Setting out chutney, crackers,
dry yellow wine, I take the fish
with a small fork from the tin.
It lies on the plate as in a still life:
stark, lean from muscling the sea,
darkened and rich with smoke.
It breaks along its inner lines
into savory morsels. Wine slows
the mind. The chutney's sweet.
I open another tin. The silver skin
is lustrous as it was lifted by net
into the chill air. It is fish salty
as the ocean itself, an ur-flavor
of the blue planet. It was shielded
amid the others: beatific, alive.
And as it might in the shark's dim
mouth, it disappears in mine.

Figs

It's mid-October, warm as a summer day.
I check the tree again: a purplish skin is ripe.
Pick it: milky sap leaks from the stem.
You rinse it and half it with a knife.
Pale wet seeds pack the fruit.
In spring the first green nodes of fig emerged
where one limb divides from another.
Pollen-smudged wasps entered them—
they learned eons ago to do it,
and so through the weeks: the future—
the harvest—arrived one moment at a time.

The airy tree grows just off the patio,
its leaves raked and gone now.
I look for mature fruit in the sun.
Frost comes soon, of course.
If I miss one, the birds won't.
They may peck at it: one divot.
It's a syrupy sweetness, the seeds
crisp, gritty between the teeth.
The seed's not viable until it's vulnerable.
Open the fig: it's like a glimpse
inside ourselves: ovary, testicle—
a rich pink inward flowering—
the possible secreted in what is.

The fig holds fast, umbilical,
hangs aloft til the precise moment:
it's released, plucked by gravity,
grounded. Ants overrun it.
A night rambler — a raccoon — gorges;
figs fit neatly in its hands.
A roothold's unlikely, a fragile appending.
Flies and last bees too are interested.
I wash summer dust off another
and slice: the tender fig does not resist.

Watching TV News with Mother:
Burmese Pythons Rule the Everglades

The enormous snake whose
far end can't be seen lies inert
in the saw grass. Open-eyed,
mute, it's sentient of what?
It is a surreal transplant
with like us no natural
predator but ourselves.
'Your years in Florida,
did you see alligators?'
She says without pause:
'I'm afraid of everything.'
She's silenced me, is surely
joking, and yet the candor
is not new. She's ninety-one
and has conquered secrecy.
Having thought it over now,
she nods, 'Everything, yes.'
Is she smiling? It's not clear
amid the lines and wrinkles.
I ask: 'What, for example?'
'What you really think of me.'

The Seeping Dream

Water in his bedroom is up to his knees.
His milk-white body unclothed, indistinct,
he — my father — gropes methodically about.
He lifts his thin legs like a wading bird.
Liquid shadows mirror-ripple the ceiling.
The small room is empty except for the bed,
his disheveled island. His tools lie there.
He's holding a wrench. Silent old man,
he gazes into the faintly stirring water.

The level's rising on the bare paneled walls —
I know this rather than see it inch its way up.
'Go ahead,' he insists. 'I'll meet you later
at the hotel, all of you,' he says, yet faces
away from me, speaking more to himself.
Crouching stiffly, he feels along the bottom.
I see the erratic churning everywhere now.
There is not one source, but surely many.

I take in the dim, low-ceilinged room again,
place of his illness, his isolation. What is it
I came here to say? I notice — how had
I not — the loin cloth, strips of old sheet.
Loosely bound, it does not fully cover
the white thatch of hair, the sleeping cock.
I'm lethargic suddenly. 'I'll be back,' I say,
'with help…a doctor,' yet know I won't.
He turns to me half-way and says good-bye,
but his smile is not connected to his voice.

Blue Wasps in November Sun

The wasp exploring empty white ceiling
half falls — a blur, flailing, crash landing.
It lies still on the open dictionary.
I too am motionless in the window's sun.
The wasp's black, lozenged eyes matched
the light before we appeared, we who
live out our desire for what it seems is
clearly, faithfully sculpted by the light.

The other wasps inside proceed about
industriously on the sunny window,
its panes filmed with summer dust.
By late afternoon, they scurry — doing
what? — to and fro across cool glass.
Their pace picks up to a near frenzy.
An open window — escape — and one
freezing night would finish them.

Now the light is amber-gold and rakes
at near the level of one's eyes and
is almost palpable. It illuminates
the bookshelf for a long moment:
in it, the books do not appear useful
in any way one had thought of them.

The wasps have slowed to a crawl.
The speed of light carries it past time —
it has no place, yet can show us ours.

I'm at the window to check the moon.
It's full, awake in late night blackness.
I draw the curtains. The wasps startle me:
dark marks secreted in a vague fold.
Holding to the cloth, they do not stir.

What the River Contains

I'm speeding, blunt bow slapping, and pass from
the cool shadows of the island's trees to the light
mid-river and the last minute of face-warming sun.
I've been upriver birding, shadowing a heron roost,
an afternoon of small, almost unnoticed pleasures.
Near the bend that gives the first glimpse of town,
I cut the motor and relax into the slow silence.
The boat's wake spreads behind me. To one side it
breaks rhythmically on the darkened island and
on the other along a bank edged with bean field,
the orderly and yellowing incarnation of summer.
The river is pale, sluggish in a rainless October.
Suddenly, far ahead as I can see, shad fingerlings
leap up, pale silver knives, up, each for an instant
airborne, flexing, hundreds in a wide, jittery swath.
Now I drift uneasily into their enormous school.
An electric joy or hunger propels them, or they
are prey — alarmed — driven into the trackless air.
They thump live against the sides of the boat.
Each erupts, flies — revealed — and then in every
angle of entry, *thup, thup,* dives, drops in again.

I pass gradually through and then beyond them
and paddle the last mile home as dusk comes on.
The cool air is empty now of the dizzy swallows.
There are lit windows in the town's waterfront.
Fragments of voices carry over the dim water,
a child's laughter. The boat tied up, I remain
and watch the sky and river all but unmasked
of light and featureless. Now and then the boat
tilts, sways a bit on mild waves. What the river
contains seems more intimate to me, if even less
translatable — or say another kind of knowledge
has accrued: a blend of memory and affection.
I have taken much from it. It can ask for nothing.
It holds nothing back. If it can be said to give,
we do nothing in return. Sky-cold rains are in it,
long, sun-warmed afternoons. Each creek and
river upstream is in it: the Allegheny, Scioto,
Big Sandy, the Tennessee: each name erased.
If an end is proposed, it too is swept along and
loses its urgency among the fish-quick shapes.
The river is capacious like the emptiness each
new instant fills — there is room for the shad
in it and for the tires and the oblivious leaves.

About the Author

DAVID POLK grew up beside the Ohio River — at the mouth of the Tennessee — where he lives now. He studied with Wendell Berry and Guy Davenport at the University of Kentucky, and has an M.F.A. from the writing program at San Francisco State University. He has taught writing and literature at many schools including the University of Cincinnati, Eastern Kentucky University, Portland Art Museum School, and served as curator of the Elliston Collection of Poetry. His work has appeared in the *Paris Review,* *Cincinnati Poetry Review,* and *Epoch* among others. The author of four books of military history, he has reviewed books and art for the *Louisville Courier-Journal* and other papers. He lived for years in the Shawnee Forest and at the mouth of the Cumberland River.

This book has been set in Adobe Jenson
a typeface designed by Robert Slimbach
based on a text face cut by Nicolas Jenson
in Venice around 1470. Its italic
are based on those created by
Ludovico Vicentino degli Arrighi
fifty years later.

Book design by
Jonathan Greene

www.ingramcontent.com/pod-product-compliance
Lightning Source LLC
Chambersburg PA
CBHW022009120526
44592CB00034B/757